# RODGERS &
## THE ILLUSTRATED SONGBOOK
# HAMMERSTEIN

D1275542

ALLSTON BRANCH LIBRARY

UNIVERSE / HAL LEONARD

AL BR
M1507
.R7
R63
1998x

Foreword by Andrew Lloyd Webber © 1998 Time, Inc. Reprinted by permission.

First published in the United States of America in 1998 by:

HAL LEONARD CORPORATION

7777 W. Bluemound Road

P.O. Box 13819

Milwaukee, WI 53213

UNIVERSE PUBLISHING

A Division of Rizzoli International Publications, Inc.

300 Park Avenue South

New York, NY 10010

Copyright © 1998 Universe Publishing/Hal Leonard Corporation

Distributed to the music trade by Hal Leonard Corporation

Distributed to the U.S. book trade by St. Martin's Press, New York

Distributed to the book trade in Canada by McClelland & Stewart

All rights reserved. No part of this publication
may be reproduced, stored in a retrieval system, or
transmitted in any form or by any means,
electronic, mechanical, photocopying, recording,
or otherwise, without prior consent of the publishers.

98 99 00 / 10 9 8 7 6 5 4 3 2 1

Library of Congress Catalog Card Number: 98-61198

Printed in the United States of America

Design by Amelia Costigan

Photo credits:

FRONT COVER: Donna Murphy and Lou Diamond Phillips in
the 1996 Broadway revival of *The King and I*. (© 1996 Joan Marcus)

FACING PAGE: Richard Rodgers and Oscar Hammerstein II.

© 1994 Joan Marcus/Marc Bryan-Brown: pp. 38, 44, 48
© 1996 Joan Marcus: pp. 106 (bottom), 107, 118, 123
© 1998 Joan Marcus: pp. 174 (top left), 175, 180

© 1995 Carol Rosegg: pp. 60, 61

Martha Swope, © Time, Inc.: pp. 15, 30

Photofest: pp. 39, 71 (bottom), 80, 129, 151, 158 (bottom left), 189

*Rodgers & Hammerstein's Cinderella* (p. 143): © Disney. All rights reserved.

*Oklahoma!* ( p. 24) courtesy of The Rodgers and Hammerstein Organization and
Metro-Goldwyn-Mayer. © 1955 Estate of Richard Rodgers and Oscar Hammerstein II. All rights reserved.

*South Pacific* (pp. 87 and 93) courtesy of The Rodgers and Hammerstein Organization and Metro-Goldwyn-Mayer. © 1958 Estate of Richard Rodgers and Oscar
Hammerstein II. All rights reserved.

*State Fair* (p. 59) © 1945 Twentieth Century Fox Film Corporation.
All rights reserved.

*The Sound of Music* (p. 173 and back cover) © 1965 Twentieth Century Fox Film
Corporation. All rights reserved.

All other photos courtesy of The Rodgers and Hammerstein Organization.

For further information on the musicals of Rodgers and Hammerstein,
including the licensing of theatrical performances, visit:

**www.rnh.com**

# Foreword
## by Andrew Lloyd Webber

It was 8:30 a.m., May 19, 1961. I remember the time and date vividly. I was thirteen. School was Westminster. Elvis was king. Number one on the British charts was Floyd Cramer's "On the Rebound." There was an uproar as I entered the common room, where we boys were supplied with the daily newspapers.

"Have you read your heroes' reviews, Lloydy?" "Look, the *Times* says the show is treacly." "Webster, look at *this* one." *That* one said something to the effect that "if you are a diabetic who craves sweet things, take along some extra insulin, and you will not fail to thrill to *The Sound of Music.*"

If nothing else, I had learned my first lesson in creative theater advertising, for "You will not fail to thrill to *The Sound of Music*" was the main quote outside London's Palace Theatre for many years to come. When the sign finally came down, Richard Rodgers and Oscar Hammerstein's last collaboration had become the longest-running American musical in London theater history. Few remember in what disregard, particularly in 1960s Britain, the musical genre was held by young people. Opinion-makers insisted that the most heinous example of the sentimental musical was the show rightly considered today to be a Rodgers and Hammerstein masterpiece, *Carousel.*

My first encounter with Rodgers and Hammerstein was via my father. He was then director of composition at the Royal College of Music. On my tenth birthday, he interrupted my endless replays of "Jailhouse Rock" and insisted on playing something for me. Onto the battered 78 r.p.m. record player was plonked Ezio Pinza singing "Some Enchanted Evening." Then Dad played the song on the piano. Right then, Rodgers and Hammerstein joined Elvis Presley and the Everly Brothers as heroes.

I know why. Great melody has always deeply affected me, and Rodgers is possibly the twentieth century's greatest tune writer. This is not to deny Hammerstein's enormous contribution. The simplicity of his lyrics is truly deceptive. Take "People Will Say We're in Love." Thousands of songs, even well-known songs, make the few rhymes for "love" sound contrived. "Don't start collecting things—/ Give me my rose and my glove./ Sweetheart, they're suspecting things—/ People will say we're in love!" does no such thing.

Rodgers and Hammerstein did not, of course, collaborate until they were well along in their careers. Rodgers was born on June 28, 1902, on New York's Long Island to a doctor and his wife. He took to music at an early age. The teenage Rodgers spent his allowance going to Saturday matinees of musicals. Thus he grew to idolize Jerome Kern.

By the time he went to Columbia University in the fall of 1919, he had already met his first collaborator, Lorenz Hart. That summer they had sold a song to producer Lew Fields for a show called *A Lonely Romeo*. (Extraordinarily, some of Rodgers's songs, to his own lyrics, appeared on Broadway even earlier, when he was sixteen.)

But it wasn't until 1925 that Rodgers and Hart had a major hit. They wrote the songs for a lighthearted revue called *The Garrick Gaieties*. Its "Manhattan" was an overnight success, and the legendary partnership was flying at last. Such songs as "The Lady Is a Tramp," "Dancing on the Ceiling," "My Heart Stood Still," and "Blue Moon" etched the duo a permanent place in theater history.

Rodgers was always keen on breaking new ground. Many believe *Pal Joey* (1940), the story of the emcee of a sleazy nightclub, to be a landmark musical. With its unscrupulous leading character and bitingly realistic view of life, the show moved the musical-comedy format into more serious territory. But even as Rodgers and Hart were taking the musical to new levels, their partnership was becoming increasingly strained. Hart was a serious drinker, and by the time of his last collaboration with Rodgers, *By Jupiter* in 1942, he was virtually an alcoholic. Rodgers was desperate. No one was more forthcoming with help than his old friend Oscar Hammerstein II.

Hammerstein was born in New York City on July 12, 1895. His father William was a theatrical manager; his grandfather Oscar I, a legendary impresario who took on the Metropolitan Opera by building his own opera house. The young Oscar was stagestruck from childhood, and by the time he attended Columbia University, he was performing and writing amateur routines. It was after the Saturday matinee of a college varsity revue that he first met Rodgers, whose older brother brought him to the show. Years later, remembering this meeting, Hammerstein wrote, "Behind the sometimes too serious face of an extraordinarily talented composer...I see a dark-eyed little boy."

Like Rodgers, Hammerstein was keen to push the boundaries of the musical, which was only slightly more sophisticated than a vaudeville revue. In the program of his 1924 Broadway show *Rose-Marie*, for instance, he and the other authors wrote that the musical numbers were too integral to the book to list separately. Three years later, with Jerome Kern, he had his biggest success with *Show Boat*, the musical he adapted from Edna Ferber's novel of the same name with the express intention of weaving songs seamlessly into a narrative about addictive gambling, alcoholism, and miscegenation. Years later, Hammerstein dealt with racial issues again in *South Pacific*.

By the time Rodgers and Hammerstein were discussing the Hart crisis, the forty-six-year-old Hammerstein was considered something of a has-been. He had a string of flops to his name. Famously, after the successful debut of *Oklahoma!* he took an advertisement in *Variety* listing all his recent catastrophes with the punch line: "I've done it before and I can do it again!" The announcement that Rodgers and Hammerstein were to collaborate on *Oklahoma!* — the Theatre Guild production based on Lynn Riggs's play *Green Grow the Lilacs* — was initially greeted with skepticism. The financial backing for *Away We Go!* (as the show was then called) proved very difficult to raise. MGM, which owned the dramatic rights, refused to make a $69,000 investment for half the profits. The word on the tryout in New Haven, Connecticut, was awful. One of Walter Winchell's informants wired the columnist: "No girls, no legs, no jokes, no chance."

But on March 31, 1943, *Oklahoma!* opened in triumph on Broadway. A show that began with a lone woman churning butter onstage to the strains of an offstage voice singing "Oh, What a Beautiful Mornin'" captivated its first-night audience. This revolutionary, naturalistic musical also changed the mainstream of the genre forever.

Rodgers and Hammerstein wrote nine musicals together. Five are legendary hits: *Oklahoma!, Carousel, South Pacific, The King and I,* and *The Sound of Music. (Flower Drum Song* was a success, but not in the same league as the golden five.) They wrote one film musical, *State Fair,* and the TV special *Cinderella,* starring Julie Andrews. They were also hugely canny producers. Irving Berlin's *Annie Get Your Gun* was but one of the works they produced that was not their own. Their flops — *Allegro, Me and Juliet,* and *Pipe Dream* — were probably a result, as much as anything, of their trying too consciously to be innovative.

What sets the great Rodgers and Hammerstein musicals apart for me is their directness and their awareness of the importance of construction in musical theater. Years ago, I played through the piano score of *South Pacific.* It is staggering how skillfully reprises are used as scene-change music that sets up a following number or underlines a previous point. It could only be the product of a hugely close relationship in which each partner sensed organically where the other, and the show, was going.

After Hammerstein's death from cancer in 1960, Rodgers valiantly plowed on. He worked with Stephen Sondheim on a musical, *Do I Hear a Waltz?* An attempt at a collaboration with Alan Jay Lerner, lyricist of *My Fair Lady,* came to nothing. I can vouch for Alan's never having had the almost puritanical discipline that Rodgers found so satisfactory in Hammerstein. Sadly, too, with one or two exceptions, the post-Hammerstein melodies paled against Rodgers's former output. Who can say why? Perhaps it was simply the lack of the right partner to provide inspiration and bring out the best in him. Musical partnerships are, after all, like marriages — built on a chemistry that is intangible, perhaps not even definable. Nearly forty years later, the partnership of Rodgers and Hammerstein has not yet been equaled. It probably never will be.

Richard Rodgers and Oscar Hammerstein II standing before the marquee of
the St. James Theatre, 1951.

# Introduction
## by Theodore S. Chapin
### President of The Rodgers and Hammerstein Organization

**M**any have assumed this book has been around forever. How could there not be a Rodgers and Hammerstein songbook, containing in one volume most of their famous and well-loved songs? The songs have appeared in books, to be sure, but not since the late 1950s has there been a deluxe edition of the best songs resulting from the joint work of Richard Rodgers and Oscar Hammerstein II. The time is right. Welcome to *Rodgers and Hammerstein: The Illustrated Songbook.*

Richard Rodgers and Oscar Hammerstein II were both New Yorkers, who grew up in middle-class neighborhoods not far from each other. The Rodgers family tended toward medicine as a profession, but they were great music lovers, and the piano was usually piled high with sheet music. On the other hand, the Hammersteins were theater people; Oscar I (grandfather of Oscar II) built theaters and was, in fact, the first real estate speculator to construct a theater at Longacre Square, now known as Times Square. As such, he really was the grandfather of Broadway and the patriarch of a theatrical dynasty which included stage managers, vaudeville entrepreneurs, and directors. The lives of the Hammerstein and the Rodgers families connected in New York City during the turn of the century; Dr. Will Rodgers, for example, was the obstetrician who delivered many a Hammerstein child. It was inevitable that the lives of Richard Rodgers and Oscar Hammerstein II would interconnect. And they did, at Columbia University, New York's most prestigious institution of higher education.

Columbia University, a place of high intellectual pursuits, appreciated show business. An annual varsity show was staged to which members of the university community could contribute, although

◀ Richard Rodgers and Oscar Hammerstein II circa 1949.

only members of the senior class were allowed to perform. Since Oscar Hammerstein II was a few years older than Richard Rodgers, he participated in the varsity show first. But Rodgers's older brother was involved in the show as well, so his music-loving younger sibling was allowed to hang around and contribute some material. It was in this forum that the writers Hammerstein and Rodgers first met; in fact, they wrote a few songs together which first appeared in these varsity shows.

Once out of Columbia both Rodgers and Hammerstein pursued separate careers writing for the musical theater. Hammerstein's inclination was toward operetta while Rodgers's was in the direction of musical comedy. They each achieved remarkable success contributing to famous shows, many of which stretched the traditional rules. Rodgers wrote *Babes in Arms, Pal Joey, The Boys From Syracuse,* and *On Your Toes,* among others, while Hammerstein's output included *Show Boat, Rose-Marie,* and *The Desert Song.* Rodgers wrote exclusively with Lorenz Hart during those years, while Hammerstein worked most often with Jerome Kern, but also with George Gershwin, Vincent Youmans, Sigmund Romberg, and Otto Harbach. Each man learned a great deal from his early collaborations. Thus the stage was set for the revolution they created in 1943 when they wrote *Oklahoma!*

A word about that revolution. My generation grew up hearing that *Oklahoma!* was a revolutionary musical. When we saw it or were part of a high school production, we wondered what was the revolution. The show seemed pretty simple and straightforward. Boy meets girl, asks her to go to a dance, but she can't decide between him and another guy. A lot of stuff happens, and they end up together. From a story standpoint it doesn't sound too revolutionary. We've learned that the revolution is in the actual creation of what we now know as the musical. Every element of the production — *every element* — ties in together to create one unified and cohesive work. Rodgers explained it well when he said that "the orchestrations sound the way the costumes look." Until *Oklahoma!* came along, a show was initiated around one element: a star, an idea, a composer's signature style, a specific format, etc. From *Oklahoma!* onward musicals made sense.

This book isn't concerned with Rodgers and Hammerstein as theater people. This is about Rodgers and Hammerstein, the songwriters. And here these two fellows proved to be extraordinary. Rodgers and Hammerstein grew up in a time when people gathered around the piano and sang. The song was the musical foundation for their craft, and the songs they wrote were able to stand separately from the shows they were written for. Later, when radio became popular, everyone listened to singers. Vaudeville and revues always included songs. And the musical vernacular for songs was fairly standard — verse, eight-bar chorus repeated in AABA form, etc. But in those pre-*Oklahoma!* collaborations, both men stretched and experimented. Listen, for example, for the lack of rhymes in "Ol' Man River." There are only three rhymes in the whole song. Why? That's what Hammerstein felt suited the character and situation. In the theater, songs must do what is demanded by the play. They are informed by the place in the show, who is singing, and what the action is. This kind of thinking became second nature to both Hammerstein and Rodgers. Dramatic situations dictated the specifics, but their genius lies in how universal those expressions actually were. For example, "Edelweiss," the last song Rodgers and Hammerstein ever wrote together and one of their most popular songs today, isn't simply about a flower. In a few carefully chosen words and notes it expresses the pathos of leaving a place. "Bless my homeland forever." Don't we all have places about which we feel a similar sentiment? We can listen to "Edelweiss" and appreciate it as a popular song entirely on its own without the context of *The Sound of Music*.

Rodgers and Hammerstein were always pleased when their songs were played and sung away from the shows. They never wrote a song outside a show with any success, and the few times they tried, they were adrift without characters and plot. But so many of their songs, written for very specific situations, live very well on their own. For instance, Frank Sinatra singing "Hello, Young Lovers" is no longer about Mrs. Anna's relationship with her long-lost husband as it is in the context of *The King and I*. Sinatra makes it universal for anyone with a great love in the past. John Coltrane playing "My Favorite Things" has nothing to do with children, nuns, and a governess. In fact, every song between these covers can be sung, played, and heard as a statement all its own. The music and the words inform each other and work wonderfully well together.

Richard Rodgers and Oscar Hammerstein II lived for their work. They loved writing, they loved the theater, and they loved producing. There is a wonderful letter from Hammerstein to Rodgers during the writing of *Cinderella;* Hammerstein was in Australia, Rodgers in New York. After seeing the film *The King and I*, Hammerstein wrote to his collaborator, then of fourteen prosperous years, that he was convinced it was their best work and would remain modern for a very long time. How right he turned out to be. The fact that the cover of this songbook is the famous "Shall We Dance?" moment from the glorious 1996 Tony-Award-winning Broadway revival of *The King and I* proves him correct.

When I was a kid, the Rodgers and Hart Songbook lived on the piano at home, providing me with my introduction to Richard Rodgers's work. Ever since coming to work at The Rodgers and Hammerstein Organization, I have hoped we could provide a special songbook that would sit on pianos and introduce new generations to the extraordinary words and music of Rodgers and Hammerstein. Now that several of the shows have been given revelatory new productions on Broadway, we can create this songbook with contemporary photographs. We can also include as a foreword the beautiful tribute written by Lord Andrew Lloyd-Webber for the 1998 *Time* Magazine/CBS-TV list of the one hundred most influential people of the twentieth century. That Rodgers and Hammerstein were chosen to be among the twenty "Artists & Entertainers" was an honor in itself. Having Lord Lloyd-Webber write about these two artists who deeply influenced him is a tribute of equal honor.

OKLAHOMA!

*Oklahoma!* based on the play *Green Grow the Lilacs* by Lynn Riggs. *Oklahoma!* opened on Broadway on March 31, 1943, at the St. James Theatre for a run of 2,212 performances.

Music by Richard Rodgers. Book and Lyrics by Oscar Hammerstein II. Directed by Rouben Mamoulian. Choreography by Agnes de Mille. Orchestrations by Robert Russell Bennett. Musical director, Jay S. Blackton. Produced by the Theatre Guild.

### PRINCIPAL ORIGINAL CAST

Curly McLain . . . . . . . . . . . . . . . . . . . . . . . . . . . . . . . . . . . . . . . . . . . . . Alfred Drake
Laurey Williams . . . . . . . . . . . . . . . . . . . . . . . . . . . . . . . . . . . . . . . . . . Joan Roberts
Ado Annie Carnes . . . . . . . . . . . . . . . . . . . . . . . . . . . . . . . . . . . . . . . . Celeste Holm
Will Parker . . . . . . . . . . . . . . . . . . . . . . . . . . . . . . . . . . . . . . . . . . . . . . . Lee Dixon
Jud Fry . . . . . . . . . . . . . . . . . . . . . . . . . . . . . . . . . . . . . . . . . . . . . Howard da Silva

**SYNOPSIS.** On the eve of the Oklahoma Territory's accession to the union, Curly McLain is courting Laurey Williams. To make her handsome cowboy jealous, the flirtatious Laurey accepts the invitation of farmhand Jud Fry to attend a box social. Meanwhile, Laurey's friend Ado Annie, a cheerful and funny girl who "cain't say no," is torn between her suitor, Will Parker, and a peddler, Ali Hakim, whose main appeal is that he talks "purty." When Laurey tries to break her date with Jud, the sinister farmhand turns nasty. After Curly boots him out of the party, Jud swears revenge and tries to set Laurey's family farm on fire. A fight between Curly and Jud ensues, with Jud accidentally killing himself on his own knife. Curly is found innocent of manslaughter and joins Laurey, Ado Annie, Will Parker, and the cowboys and farmers in a celebration of the newborn state of Oklahoma.

**p. 13:** Marc Platt and Katherine Sergava as Dream Laurey and Dream Curly in the "Dream Ballet" from the original 1943 Broadway production of *Oklahoma!*.

**p. 14:** ABOVE: The original show poster for *Oklahoma!*. BELOW: Jud Fry's "postcard girls" in the "Dream Ballet" from the original 1943 Broadway production.

**p. 15:** TOP: Harry Groener leads "The Farmer and the Cowman Should Be Friends" from the 1979 Broadway revival. BOTTOM: Christine Andreas as Laurey and Laurence Guittard as Curly in the 1979 Broadway revival of *Oklahoma!*.

**COMMENTARY.** In deciding to collaborate for the first time on a musical, Richard Rodgers and Oscar Hammerstein II, both then in their forties, entered a completely new phase of their creative careers. Rodgers discovered in Hammerstein a collaborator whose naturalistic sensitivity urged from him a new, freely expressive musical style as a composer. For his part, Hammerstein found in Rodgers a composer whose music seemed the perfect complement to his own lyricism. At the time of writing *Oklahoma!*, though, neither initially foresaw that their collaboration would become permanent.

Rodgers and Hammerstein spent weeks discussing every artistic and practical aspect of what would become *Oklahoma!* before even one song was written. The new collaboration also marked a change of working habits for Richard Rodgers. In the past he always wrote the music first, and then Lorenz Hart, his partner of twenty-five years, would write lyrics to suit the tune. Hammerstein had worked in that manner when necessary (especially with Jerome Kern), but preferred to write his lyrics first, usually spending a great amount of time polishing them.

Nothing prepared those first audiences of 1943 for what they saw in the ground-breaking *Oklahoma!*. In previous decades, with a few notable exceptions, musicals were known for the lightness of their largely incongruous books, the prevailing argument being that audiences came to enjoy the songs and dances, and if they wanted a heavy storyline they would attend a straight play. What characterized *Oklahoma!* was the seemingly perfect integration of character, story, music, and dance into a cohesive whole.

*Oklahoma!* ran on Broadway for over five years and held the crown as Broadway's longest-running show until the early 1960s. A National Tour, launched in October of 1943, played for an astounding ten and a half years, visiting nearly every state in the union. The original London production opened on April 29, 1947, at the legendary Theatre Royal, Drury Lane, and became the longest-running show in that theater's 270-year history, eventually playing for a total of 1,548 performances. The 1955 movie version, starring Shirley Jones and Gordon MacRae, and the thousands of community, school, stock, and professional revivals since have ensured its place as America's most popular folk musical. Among its honors were a special Pulitzer Prize, a special Tony Award, a special Grammy Award, and two Academy Awards. In 1993, on the occasion of its fiftieth anniversary, *Oklahoma!* was commemorated with a United States postage stamp, the first Broadway show so honored.

# OH, WHAT A BEAUTIFUL MORNIN'

Lyrics by OSCAR HAMMERSTEIN II

Music by RICHARD RODGERS

**Moderate Waltz**

There's a

bright gold - en haze on the mead - ow, _____
cat - tle are stand - in' like stat - ues, _____
sounds of the earth are like mu - sic, _____

_____ there's a bright gold - en haze on the mead - ow.
_____ all the cat - tle are stand - in' like stat - ues.
_____ all the sounds of the earth are like mu - sic.

Copyright © 1943 by WILLIAMSON MUSIC
Copyright Renewed
International Copyright Secured  All Rights Reserved

# PEOPLE WILL SAY WE'RE IN LOVE

Lyrics by OSCAR HAMMERSTEIN II

Music by RICHARD RODGERS

Copyright © 1943 by WILLIAMSON MUSIC
Copyright Renewed
International Copyright Secured   All Rights Reserved

Gordon MacRae and Shirley Jones as Curly and Laurey in the 1955 movie production.

# THE SURREY WITH THE FRINGE ON TOP

Lyrics by OSCAR HAMMERSTEIN II

Music by RICHARD RODGERS

Copyright © 1943 by WILLIAMSON MUSIC
Copyright Renewed
International Copyright Secured   All Rights Reserved

The finale from the 1979 Broadway revival.

# OKLAHOMA

Lyrics by OSCAR HAMMERSTEIN II

Music by RICHARD RODGERS

Copyright © 1943 by WILLIAMSON MUSIC
Copyright Renewed
International Copyright Secured   All Rights Reserved

CAROUSEL

*Carousel* based on the play *Liliom* by Ferenc Molnar, as adapted by Benjamin F. Glaser. *Carousel* opened on Broadway on April 19, 1945, at the Majestic Theatre for a run of 890 performances.

Music by Richard Rodgers. Book and Lyrics by Oscar Hammerstein II. Directed by Rouben Mamoulian. Choreography by Agnes de Mille. Orchestrations by Don Walker. Musical director, Joseph Littau. Produced by the Theatre Guild.

### PRINCIPAL ORIGINAL CAST

| | |
|---|---|
| Julie Jordan | Jan Clayton |
| Billy Bigelow | John Raitt |
| Carrie Pipperidge | Jean Darling |
| Enoch Snow | Eric Mattson |
| Nettie Fowler | Christine Johnson |

**SYNOPSIS.** In 1873 on the New England coast, Billy Bigelow, a carousel barker, and Julie Jordan, a young factory worker, fall in love and marry. Billy is out of work, and the couple moves in with Julie's cousin, Nettie Fowler. Unable to find a job, Billy takes his frustrations out on his young wife. When Julie becomes pregnant, Billy, feeling desperate, is tempted by a hoodlum into committing a robbery. He is captured, but takes his own life rather than being taken prisoner, leaving Julie alone with an unborn child. In heaven Billy is allowed one day back on Earth to right his wrongs. It is now fifteen years later. Billy's teenage daughter, Louise, is a lonely, troubled girl, suffering from her father's wrongs and his absence. Billy tries to tell her good things about her dead father, and she wants to believe him, but becomes suspicious when he gives her a star which he brought with him from heaven. Julie finds the star and seems to understand Billy's presence. Later, at Louise's school graduation, the unseen Billy, through unselfish love, wills his wife and daughter to have hope in their futures.

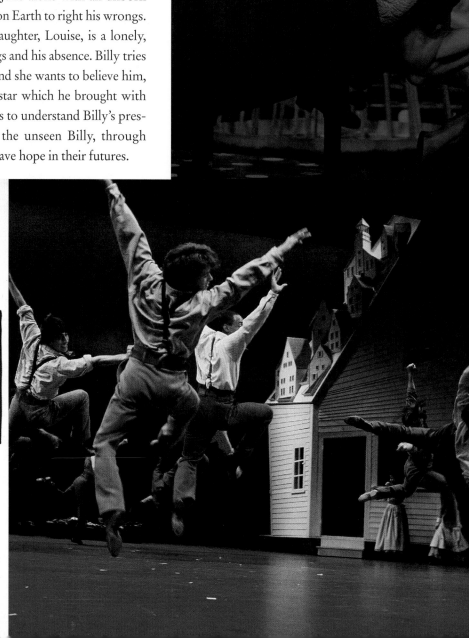

# Carousel

*A New Musical Play*

Based on FERENC MOLNAR'S "LILIOM" as adapted by Benjamin F. Glazer

**Music by RICHARD RODGERS**
**Book and Lyrics by OSCAR HAMMERSTEIN 2d**
**Directed by ROUBEN MAMOULIAN**
**Dances by AGNES DE MILLE**
Settings by JO MIELZINER

*with*

JOHN RAITT • JAN CLAYTON
Christine Johnson • Eric Mattson • Jean Casto
*and a Bright Young Cast of Singers and Dancers*

**COMMENTARY.** *Carousel* had essentially the same creative team as did *Oklahoma!*. At first Rodgers and Hammerstein were reluctant to tackle Molnar's play, but saw the possibilities when Hammerstein moved the setting from Hungary to the New England coast. He later wrote, "I began to see an attractive ensemble. The sailors, whalers, girls who worked in the mills up the river, clambakes on nearby islands, and an amusement park on the seaboard. I saw people who were alive and lusty, people who had always been depicted onstage as thin-lipped Puritans, which was a libel." Rodgers decided to break with tradition, and instead of the standard overture he wrote a waltz that evoked the carousel of the title and the amusement park in which the opening scene is set. In another innovation in his personal style, he created expansive, operatic numbers for the score.

In a striking repeat of the situation that had benefitted *Oklahoma!* so well, the creative team also resisted the idea of hiring name stars. Instead they cast John Raitt, who had played Curly in the national tour of *Oklahoma!*, as Billy Bigelow, and Jan Clayton, a native of Los Angeles who had never appeared on Broadway, to portray Julie.

After opening in New York to rapturous critical acclaim, *Carousel* opened in London on June 7, 1950, playing 566 performances. In 1956 a gorgeous screen version was released, starring Gordon MacRae and Shirley Jones. (Frank Sinatra was to play Billy, but pulled out of the film.) An award-winning revival, with a stunning new design, opened in London in 1993 and on Broadway in 1994, where it starred Michael Hayden, Sally Murphy, Audra Ann McDonald, and opera star Shirley Verrett.

Until the end of his life, Richard Rodgers cherished the score of *Carousel* as the best music he'd ever written.

**p. 37**: Jan Clayton and John Raitt as Julie Jordan and Billy Bigelow in the original 1945 Broadway production of *Carousel*.

**p. 38**: TOP: Sally Murphy and Michael Hayden as Julie Jordan and Billy Bigelow in the 1994 Broadway revival. BOTTOM LEFT: The original show poster for *Carousel*. BOTTOM RIGHT: "June is Bustin' Out All Over" from the 1994 Broadway revival.

**p. 39**: Jan Clayton and John Raitt in the original 1945 Broadway production.

# IF I LOVED YOU

Lyrics by OSCAR HAMMERSTEIN II

Music by RICHARD RODGERS

**Allegretto moderato**

When I worked in the mill, Weav-in' at the loom, I'd gaze ab-sent-
Kind-a scraw-ny and pale, Pick-in' at my food And love-sick like

mind-ed at the roof _____ And half the time the shut-tle 'd
an-y oth-er guy _____ I'd throw a-way my sweat-er and

tan-gle in the threads, And the warp 'd get mixed with the woof _____
dress up like a dude in a dick-ey and a col-lar and a tie _____

Copyright © 1945 by WILLIAMSON MUSIC
Copyright Renewed
International Copyright Secured   All Rights Reserved

Michael Hayden and Sally Murphy in the 1994 Broadway revival of *Carousel*.

# YOU'LL NEVER WALK ALONE

Lyrics by OSCAR HAMMERSTEIN II

Music by RICHARD RODGERS

Andantino molto cantabile

*(with great warmth, like a hymn)*

* alternate lyric: hold your head up high

Copyright © 1945 by WILLIAMSON MUSIC
Copyright Renewed
International Copyright Secured   All Rights Reserved

Billy meets Julie as the carousel comes to life in the revelatory opening sequence from the 1994 Broadway revival.

# WHEN THE CHILDREN ARE ASLEEP

Lyrics by OSCAR HAMMERSTEIN II

Music by RICHARD RODGERS

Copyright © 1945 by WILLIAMSON MUSIC
Copyright Renewed
International Copyright Secured   All Rights Reserved

**Refrain**

When the chil-dren are a-sleep, we'll sit and dream _____

_____ The things that ev - 'ry oth-er dad and moth-er

dream. _____ When the chil-dren are a-sleep and lights are

low, _____ If I still love you the way I

# JUNE IS BUSTIN' OUT ALL OVER

Lyrics by OSCAR HAMMERSTEIN II

Music by RICHARD RODGERS

Copyright © 1945 by WILLIAMSON MUSIC
Copyright Renewed
International Copyright Secured   All Rights Reserved

STATE FAIR

p. 59: Jeanne Crain in the 1945 film version of *State Fair*.

p. 60–61: ABOVE LEFT: John Davidson, Ben Wright, Kathryn Crosby, and Andrea McArdle in the 1996 Broadway production of *State Fair*. ABOVE RIGHT: Vintage sheet music for the Academy-Award- winning Best Song of 1945, "It Might as Well Be Spring." BELOW AND FACING PAGE: Scenes from the 1996 Broadway production.

*State Fair* (film) based on the novel by Phil Stong. *State Fair* was released on August 20, 1945.

Music by Richard Rodgers. Screenplay and Lyrics by Oscar Hammerstein II. Adapted by Sonya Levien and Paul Green. Orchestrations by Edward Powell. Directed by Walter Lang. Produced by Twentieth Century Fox.

## PRINCIPAL ORIGINAL CAST

Margy Frake . . . . . . . . . . . . . . . . . . . . . . . . . . . . . . . . . . . Jeanne Crain
(sung by Louanne Hogan)
Pat Gilbert . . . . . . . . . . . . . . . . . . . . . . . . . . . . . . . Dana Andrews
Wayne Frake . . . . . . . . . . . . . . . . . . . . . . . . . . . . . . . . Dick Haymes
Emily Edwards . . . . . . . . . . . . . . . . . . . . . . . . . . . . . . Vivian Blaine
Abel Frake . . . . . . . . . . . . . . . . . . . . . . . . . . . . . Charles Winninger
Melissa Frake . . . . . . . . . . . . . . . . . . . . . . . . . . . . . . . . Fay Bainter

SYNOPSIS. The Frake family — Abel, his wife Melissa, their upstanding son, Wayne, and his restless and romantic sister, Margy — live on a farm near Brunswick, Iowa. They make their annual visit to the Iowa State Fair in Des Moines. Abel wins a prize for his hog, and Melissa wins a blue ribbon for her mincemeat. Margy has a romance with a newspaper reporter and Wayne is taken with a flashy dance band singer. After a week in the city, the Frakes go back home, but Margy has found true love.

**COMMENTARY.** With *Oklahoma!* running on Broadway, Rodgers and Hammerstein accepted a commission from Twentieth Century Fox to score a musical screen treatment of *State Fair*, which the studio had filmed as a non-musical in 1933. In their contract the writers stipulated that they wouldn't be required to go to Hollywood to work on the film, since neither cared for working in California.

The plot enabled them to create a score that echoed the earthy, rural tones of *Oklahoma!* and was bathed in the same kind of homespun humor. "It's a Grand Night for Singing" and "It Might as Well Be Spring" fast became standards, with the latter receiving the Oscar for Best Original Song.

The film was so successful that the studio decided to do a second version, released in 1962, starring Pat Boone and Ann-Margret. This time the setting was moved to the Texas State Fair, and Rodgers was persuaded to write five new songs, for which he wrote the lyrics himself. (Nevertheless, he didn't think much of the later screen version.) But that's not the end of the *State Fair* story. The show was adapted for the stage and in 1996 opened on Broadway, starring John Davidson, Andrea McArdle, Kathryn Crosby, and Donna McKechnie. As a result, more than fifty years after they wrote *State Fair*, Rodgers and Hammerstein received a Tony nomination for Best Original Score.

# IT'S A GRAND NIGHT FOR SINGING

Lyrics by OSCAR HAMMERSTEIN II

Music by RICHARD RODGERS

Copyright © 1945 by WILLIAMSON MUSIC
Copyright Renewed
International Copyright Secured   All Rights Reserved

# IT MIGHT AS WELL BE SPRING

Lyrics by OSCAR HAMMERSTEIN II

Music by RICHARD RODGERS

Copyright © 1945 by WILLIAMSON MUSIC
Copyright Renewed
International Copyright Secured   All Rights Reserved

ALLEGRO

*Allegro* opened on Broadway on October 10, 1947, at the Majestic Theatre for a run of 315 performances.

Music by Richard Rodgers. Book and Lyrics by Oscar Hammerstein II. Direction and Choreography by Agnes de Mille. Orchestrations by Robert Russell Bennett. Musical director, Salvatore Dell'Isola. Produced by the Theatre Guild.

## PRINCIPAL ORIGINAL CAST

Joseph Taylor, Jr. . . . . . . . . . . . . . . . . . . . . . . . . . . . . . . . . .John Battles
Marjorie Taylor . . . . . . . . . . . . . . . . . . . . . . . . . . . .Annamary Dickey
Charlie Townsend . . . . . . . . . . . . . . . . . . . . . . . . . . . . . . .John Conte
Ned Brinker . . . . . . . . . . . . . . . . . . . . . . . . . . . . . . . . . . . . . .Paul Parks
Beulah . . . . . . . . . . . . . . . . . . . . . . . . . . . . . . . . . . . . . . .Gloria Wills
Emily West . . . . . . . . . . . . . . . . . . . . . . . . . . . . . . . . . . . . . .Lisa Kirk

**SYNOPSIS.** The story starts in 1905 on the day Joseph Taylor, Jr. is born and follows his life to his thirty-fifth year. The three major locations of action, all in the same midwestern state, are his hometown, where we see him grow up, his college town, and a large city, where he becomes a successful doctor on staff at a hospital. Both big-city pressures and hospital politics make Joe lose sight of his values. After an epiphany he returns to his hometown to open a private practice with the nurse who has always loved him.

**COMMENTARY.** By the standards Rodgers and Hammerstein had established for themselves, *Allegro* must be counted as a failure, but an experimental and honest one done on their own terms. For many years Hammerstein had wanted to write an original musical tracing a man's life from cradle to grave. Eventually, it was agreed to limit the span from his birth to his mid-thirties.

There was no scenery in the conventional sense. The ensemble was used as a Greek chorus, commenting on the actions and emotions of the characters. Audiences who had been swept off their feet by *Oklahoma!* and *Carousel* didn't know what to make of this unusual allegory, although critics did appreciate the show's artistic aims. In view of the direction the American musical has taken in more recent years, *Allegro* now appears to have been way ahead of its time. Rodgers and Hammerstein themselves often expressed the hope that they might one day be able to return to the musical, but never got the chance.

p. 70: Kathryn Lee and Harrison Muller in the 1947 Broadway production of *Allegro*.

p. 71: ABOVE: John Conte and two chorus girls. BELOW: The program cover from the Broadway production.

p. 72: Kathryn Lee and male chorus.

# THE GENTLEMAN IS A DOPE

Lyrics by OSCAR HAMMERSTEIN II

Music by RICHARD RODGERS

Copyright © 1947 by Richard Rodgers and Oscar Hammerstein II
Copyright Renewed
WILLIAMSON MUSIC owner of publication and allied rights throughout the world
International Copyright Secured   All Rights Reserved

SOUTH PACIFIC

*South Pacific* adapted from *Tales of the South Pacific* by James Michener. *South Pacific* opened on Broadway on April 7, 1949, at the Majestic Theatre for a run of 1,925 performances.

Music by Richard Rodgers. Lyrics by Oscar Hammerstein II. Book by Oscar Hammerstein II and Joshua Logan. Directed by Joshua Logan. Orchestrations by Robert Russell Bennett. Musical director, Salvatore Dell'Isola. Produced by Rodgers and Hammerstein.

### PRINCIPAL ORIGINAL CAST

Ensign Nellie Forbush . . . . . . . . . . . . . . . . . . . . . . . . . . . Mary Martin .
Emile de Becque . . . . . . . . . . . . . . . . . . . . . . . . . . . . . . . . Ezio Pinza
Bloody Mary . . . . . . . . . . . . . . . . . . . . . . . . . . . . . . . . . Juanita Hall
Lt. Joseph Cable, U.S.M.C. . . . . . . . . . . . . . . . . . . . William Tabbert
Liat . . . . . . . . . . . . . . . . . . . . . . . . . . . . . . . . . . . . . Betta St. John
Luther Billis . . . . . . . . . . . . . . . . . . . . . . . . . . . . . Myron McCormick

**SYNOPSIS.** During World War II the U.S. Navy and Marines have set up a temporary base on a remote island in the South Pacific. Ensign Nellie Forbush, a navy nurse from Little Rock, falls in love with the distinguished Emile de Becque, a French planter, who for some years has been living on the island paradise. Lt. Joe Cable is a newly arrived officer who becomes enamored with Liat, daughter of Bloody Mary, the colorful and bawdy local woman who sells items to the troops. Nellie's southern upbringing fills her with strong prejudices about Emile's late wife and his half-Polynesian children. Joe works through the same feelings in his love for Liat, but realizes he's free of the bigotry he's been taught and now is able to follow his heart. Cable's mission is to infiltrate the nearby islands and gather enemy intelligence reports. He persuades de Becque, who knows the area better than any of them, to join the Allied cause and go with him. Cable is killed. Though no word comes about him, Nellie believes that de Becque, too, is

**p. 79:** "Some Enchanted Evening": Mary Martin as Nellie Forbush and Ezio Pinza as Emile de Becque from the original 1949 Broadway production of *South Pacific*.

**p. 80:** ABOVE: Mary Martin and Ezio Pinza in a scene from the original production. ABOVE LEFT: Richard Rodgers and Oscar Hammerstein II with Mary Martin, Janet Blair (star of the national tour), and Martha Wright (Ms. Martin's Broadway successor) on the closing night of the Broadway run.

dead and regrets her reluctance to accept a life with him. She goes to his house to comfort his small children, but soon Emile safely returns.

**COMMENTARY.** Joshua Logan, director of *South Pacific,* initially suggested to Richard Rodgers a musicalization of "Fo' Dolla'," one of the stories from James Michener's Pulitzer-Prize -winning book. Rodgers loved the idea, but he and Hammerstein soon realized they needed to fill out the concept, so they chose another story

RICHARD RODGERS and OSCAR HAMMERSTEIN, 2nd
*present in association with*
LELAND HAYWARD & JOSHUA LOGAN

MARY      EZIO
MARTIN     PINZA

*in the Pulitzer Prize Musical Play*

# South Pacific

Music by RICHARD RODGERS
Lyrics by OSCAR HAMMERSTEIN 2nd
Book by OSCAR HAMMERSTEIN 2nd and JOSHUA LOGAN

Another innovation was to dispense with conventional choreography for all the musical numbers, focusing instead on the characters and the storytelling.

The secondary plot about a young American officer who falls in love with an attractive native girl enabled Hammerstein to once again reveal his deep sense of humanity in "You've Got to Be Carefully Taught," in which Lt. Cable expresses his awareness of the racial ills in America.

America was ripe to revisit the war experience, which ultimately had been a great victory despite devastating losses. *South Pacific* registered the highest advance sales in Broadway history before its opening. A Pulitzer Prize and nine Tony Awards only confirmed its popularity. A London edition, also starring Mary Martin, opened on November 1, 1951, and played 802 performances. In 1958, *South Pacific* was transferred to the big screen, with Mitzi Gaynor and Rossano Brazzi in the principal roles.

p. 81: ABOVE LEFT: "I'm Gonna Wash That Man Right Outa My Hair": Mary Martin in the unforgettable shampoo routine. ABOVE RIGHT: Detail from the original show poster for *South Pacific*. BOTTOM RIGHT: Mary Martin in her "Honeybun" costume from *South Pacific*. This copy autographed to Richard Rodgers: "Dick — See! You're my honeybun *today* and every *day* — Love, Mary." BOTTOM LEFT: Mary Martin and Ezio Pinza in a scene from the original production.

from the collection, "Our Heroine," and ingeniously combined the two tales into what would become *South Pacific*.

As luck would have it, about that same time Metropolitan Opera star Ezio Pinza was retiring from the opera stage and wanted to find a Broadway musical in which to star. It was Rodgers who heard this news and quickly realized they had their Emile de Becque. Rodgers and Hammerstein recently had seen Mary Martin on tour in *Annie Get Your Gun* (which they produced) and were sure they had found their Nellie, even if it took some convincing to get Martin to agree to sing on stage with Pinza. ("What do you want, two basses?" she is said to have quipped when first approached.) The writers solved the problem by allowing both stars to appear in duet scenes, but only to sing together briefly.

# SOME ENCHANTED EVENING

Lyrics by OSCAR HAMMERSTEIN II

Music by RICHARD RODGERS

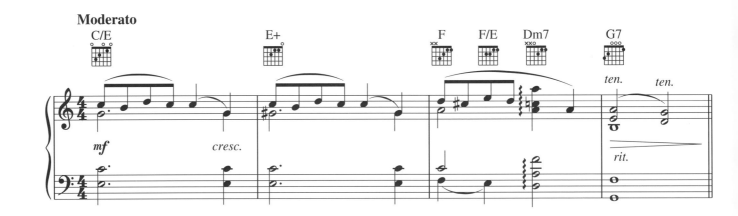

Some en-chant-ed eve-ning _____ You may see a stran-ger, _____

_____ You may see a stran-ger _____ A-cross a

Copyright © 1949 by Richard Rodgers and Oscar Hammerstein II
Copyright Renewed
WILLIAMSON MUSIC owner of publication and allied rights throughout the world
International Copyright Secured   All Rights Reserved

Rossano Brazzi and Mitzi Gaynor in the 1958 film version.

# BALI HA'I

Lyrics by OSCAR HAMMERSTEIN II

Music by RICHARD RODGERS

Most peo-ple live on a lone-ly is - land

Lost in the mid-dle of a fog-gy sea.

Most peo-ple long for an-oth-er is - land

One where they know they would like to be.

Copyright © 1949 by Richard Rodgers and Oscar Hammerstein II
Copyright Renewed
WILLIAMSON MUSIC owner of publication and allied rights throughout the world
International Copyright Secured   All Rights Reserved

Juanita Hall as Bloody Mary and John Kerr as Lt. Cable in the 1958 film.

# A WONDERFUL GUY

Lyrics by OSCAR HAMMERSTEIN II

Music by RICHARD RODGERS

Copyright © 1949 by Richard Rodgers and Oscar Hammerstein II
Copyright Renewed
WILLIAMSON MUSIC owner of publication and allied rights throughout the world
International Copyright Secured   All Rights Reserved

96

Ezio Pinza, Barbra Luna, and Noel DeLeon in the original Broadway production.

# YOUNGER THAN SPRINGTIME

Lyrics by OSCAR HAMMERSTEIN II

Music by RICHARD RODGERS

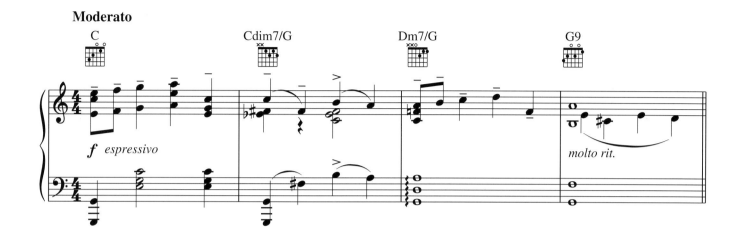

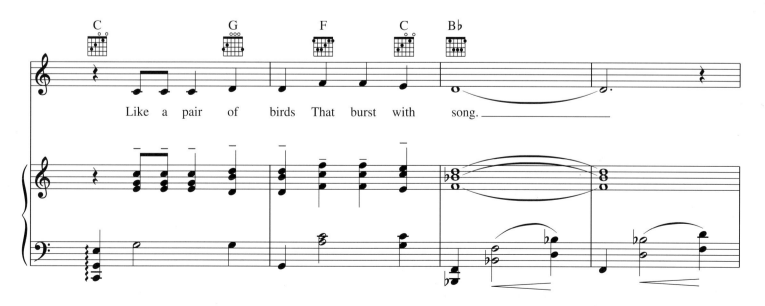

Copyright © 1949 by Richard Rodgers and Oscar Hammerstein II
Copyright Renewed
WILLIAMSON MUSIC owner of publication and allied rights throughout the world
International Copyright Secured   All Rights Reserved

THE KING AND I

*The King and I* based on the novel *Anna and the King of Siam* by Margaret Landon. *The King and I* opened on Broadway March 29, 1951, at the St. James Theatre for a run of 1,246 performances.

Music by Richard Rodgers. Book and Lyrics by Oscar Hammerstein II. Directed by John van Druten. Choreography by Jerome Robbins. Orchestrations by Robert Russell Bennett. Musical director, Frederick Dvonch. Produced by Rodgers and Hammerstein.

## PRINCIPAL ORIGINAL CAST

Anna Leonowens . . . . . . . . . . . . . . . . . . . . . . . . . . . . Gertrude Lawrence
The King . . . . . . . . . . . . . . . . . . . . . . . . . . . . . . . . . . . . . . Yul Brynner
Tuptim . . . . . . . . . . . . . . . . . . . . . . . . . . . . . . . . . Doretta Morrow
Lady Thiang . . . . . . . . . . . . . . . . . . . . . . . . . . . Dorothy Sarnoff
Lun Tha . . . . . . . . . . . . . . . . . . . . . . . . . . . . . . . . . . . Larry Douglas

**SYNOPSIS.** In the early 1860s, English school teacher Anna Leonowens, a young widow, and her son, Louis, arrive in Bangkok, where Anna is to teach the children and wives of the King of Siam. Immediately, however, the very proper yet independent Anna finds herself at odds with the King, who rules with an iron fist, resulting in frequent clashes between them. After the King seems to renege on a promise he has made to provide a house for her and her son outside of the palace, Anna embarks on a campaign to hold him to his word. Through their platonic relationship, with hints of romance, this very traditional Asian monarch makes earnest attempts to learn modern Western ways and ideas from his English schoolmistress. Anna takes under her protection Tuptim, a young woman who has been offered as a gift to the King by the Prince of Burma, and her lover Lun Tha. When Tuptim tries to escape, Lun Tha is killed, and Anna revolts deciding to leave what she sees as a barbaric place. The King, though, is dying and asks her to stay and continue to advise his young son and successor, Prince Chulalongkorn.

p. 105: "Shall We Dance?": Yul Brynner as the King of Siam and Gertrude Lawrence as Anna Leonowens in the original 1951 Broadway production of *The King and I*.

p.106: ABOVE: Yul Brynner in the original 1951 Broadway production. BELOW LEFT: Donna Murphy as Anna Leonowens in the 1996 Broadway revival. BELOW RIGHT: Detail from the original show poster for *The King and I*.

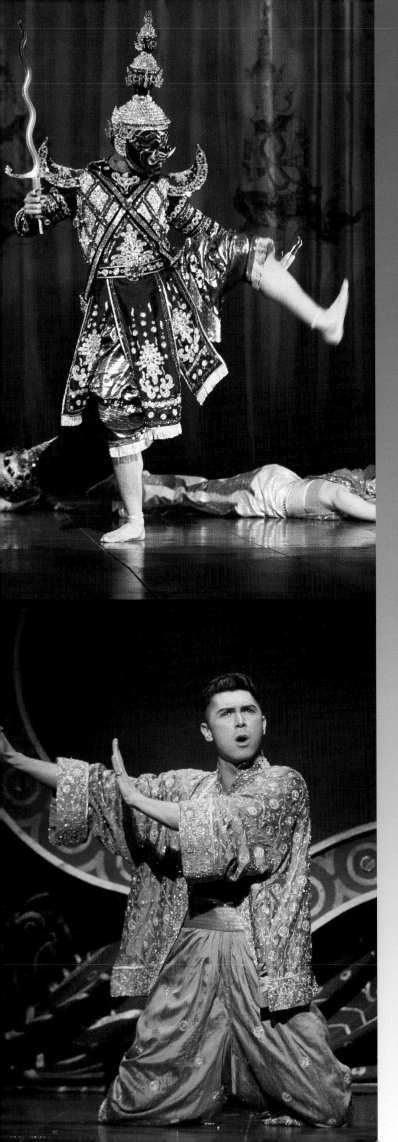

**COMMENTARY.** By 1951 Rodgers and Hammerstein were the uncontested masters of musical theater. They were poised to outdo themselves and did with their next project, based on Margaret Landon's novel, already the source of a successful stage play and film.

*The King and I* was written for legendary performer Gertrude Lawrence. (Tragically, Miss Lawrence became ill and died in 1952 during the Broadway run.) Casting the King was much more problematic. Rex Harrison and Alfred Drake both turned down the role. (Drake later played the role on Broadway.) After lengthy auditions the creators eventually settled on Yul Brynner, an obscure folk-singer "with a bony, oriental face." As Rodgers reminisced in his autobiography, "[Brynner] looked savage, he sounded savage, and there was no denying that he projected a feeling of controlled ferocity."

Once again, the grueling process of honing down the work began for the two men and their cast. In writing his opulent score, Rodgers consciously avoided using Asian instruments or anything that might sound alien to Broadway theatergoers, wisely noting, "If a composer is to reach his audience emotionally…he must reach the people through the sounds they can relate to." As for Hammerstein, he once again plumbed the depths of his own poetic sensitivity, and came up with magnificent lyrics.

Despite the awesome task of following on the success of *South Pacific, The King and I* triumphed, nevertheless, and opened to rave reviews. The show opened in London in 1953, for a run of 926 performances. In 1956 it was brought to the screen in a sumptuous version starring Yul Brynner and Deborah Kerr (singing dubbed by Marni Nixon). Throughout the years the musical was revived several times on Broadway with Brynner as the King; eventually his reign totalled over 4,625 performances! *The King and I* has enjoyed numerous revivals in the years since Brynner's death, proving that the work could outlast such a seminal star. A 1996 Broadway production starred Donna Murphy and Lou Diamond Phillips and earned four Tony Awards, including Best Musical Revival.

ABOVE: Tito Abeleda as "Simon of Legree" in the ballet, *Small House of Uncle Thomas* in the 1996 Broadway revival. LEFT: Lou Diamond Phillips as the King in the 1996 Broadway revival.

# HELLO, YOUNG LOVERS

Lyrics by OSCAR HAMMERSTEIN II

Music by RICHARD RODGERS

Copyright © 1951 by Richard Rodgers and Oscar Hammerstein II
Copyright Renewed
WILLIAMSON MUSIC owner of publication and allied rights throughout the world
International Copyright Secured   All Rights Reserved

110

# SOMETHING WONDERFUL

Lyrics by OSCAR HAMMERSTEIN II

Music by RICHARD RODGERS

Copyright © 1951 by Richard Rodgers and Oscar Hammerstein II
Copyright Renewed
WILLIAMSON MUSIC owner of publication and allied rights throughout the world
International Copyright Secured   All Rights Reserved

Donna Murphy with the Royal Children in the 1996 Broadway revival.

# GETTING TO KNOW YOU

Lyrics by OSCAR HAMMERSTEIN II

Music by RICHARD RODGERS

Copyright © 1951 by Richard Rodgers and Oscar Hammerstein II
Copyright Renewed
WILLIAMSON MUSIC owner of publication and allied rights throughout the world
International Copyright Secured   All Rights Reserved

"Shall We Dance?": Donna Murphy shows Lou Diamond Phillips some fancy footwork in the 1996 Broadway revival.

# SHALL WE DANCE?

Lyrics by OSCAR HAMMERSTEIN II

Music by RICHARD RODGERS

Copyright © 1951 by Richard Rodgers and Oscar Hammerstein II
Copyright Renewed
WILLIAMSON MUSIC owner of publication and allied rights throughout the world
International Copyright Secured   All Rights Reserved

Shall we then say "good-night" and mean "good-bye?" Or, per-chance _____ when the last lit-tle star has left the sky. Shall we still be to-geth-er with our arms a-round each

Eb  Ebmaj7  Eb6  Eb  Ab6  Bb7  Eb

# ME AND JULIET

*Me and Juliet* opened on Broadway on May 28, 1953, at the Majestic Theatre for a run of 358 performances.

Music by Richard Rodgers. Book and Lyrics by Oscar Hammerstein II. Directed by George Abbott. Choreography by Robert Alton. Orchestrations and vocal arrangements by Don Walker. Musical director, Salvatore Dell'Isola. Produced by Rodgers and Hammerstein.

## PRINCIPAL ORIGINAL CAST

| | |
|---|---|
| Jeanie | Isabel Bigley |
| Larry | Bill Hayes |
| Bob | Mark Dawson |
| Mac | Ray Walston |
| Betty Loraine | Joan McCracken |
| Charlie Clay | Arthur Maxwell |

**SYNOPSIS.** Jeanie is a chorus girl in a hit musical called *Me and Juliet.* Larry is the assistant stage manager in love with her. They secretly marry, but Bob, the stage electrician for the show, is also in love with Jeanie. When Bob discovers their marriage, he nearly kills them both in a drunken rage. But this isn't the only backstage romance in this show. Mac, the stage manager, has been seeing Betty, a dancer from another show. Suddenly Betty is cast into *Me and Juliet,* which confounds Mac, who lives by a credo never to mix romance with the show he's working on. He solves it by switching to another show himself, which allows Larry the happy ending of being promoted to stage manager. Throughout the musical, scenes from *Me and Juliet* appear in this show-within-a-show story.

**COMMENTARY.** The concept behind *Me and Juliet* seemed intriguing enough: a musical that would take place entirely inside a theater. It was a daring idea with unique challenges. Rodgers and Hammerstein set out to create a show, admittedly an unabashed valentine to the theater, with an original story that would return to the simpler tradition of song-and-dance musical comedy. The hit musical inside the show was the framework for a backstage romance.

In the year prior to *Me and Juliet,* Richard Rodgers had scored the background music to a twenty-six-part NBC television documentary series about the U.S. Navy's sea battles during World War II, *Victory at Sea.* A particularly

catchy tune from that score was a slow tango, "Beneath the Southern Cross." Rodgers liked it so much that he found a place for it in *Me and Juliet,* and with lyrics it became "No Other Love."

However well-intended, the show didn't succeed. Rodgers later stated, "Whatever flickering optimism any one of us may have had about *Me and Juliet* was quickly doused when we heard people raving about the sets, without a word being said about the rest of the show."

**p. 128:** Isabel Bigley as Jeanie and Bill Hayes as Larry from the 1953 Broadway production of *Me and Juliet.*

**p. 129:** Isabel Bigley and Bill Hayes.

**p. 130:** Joan McCracken as Betty Loraine in a scene from *Me and Juliet.*

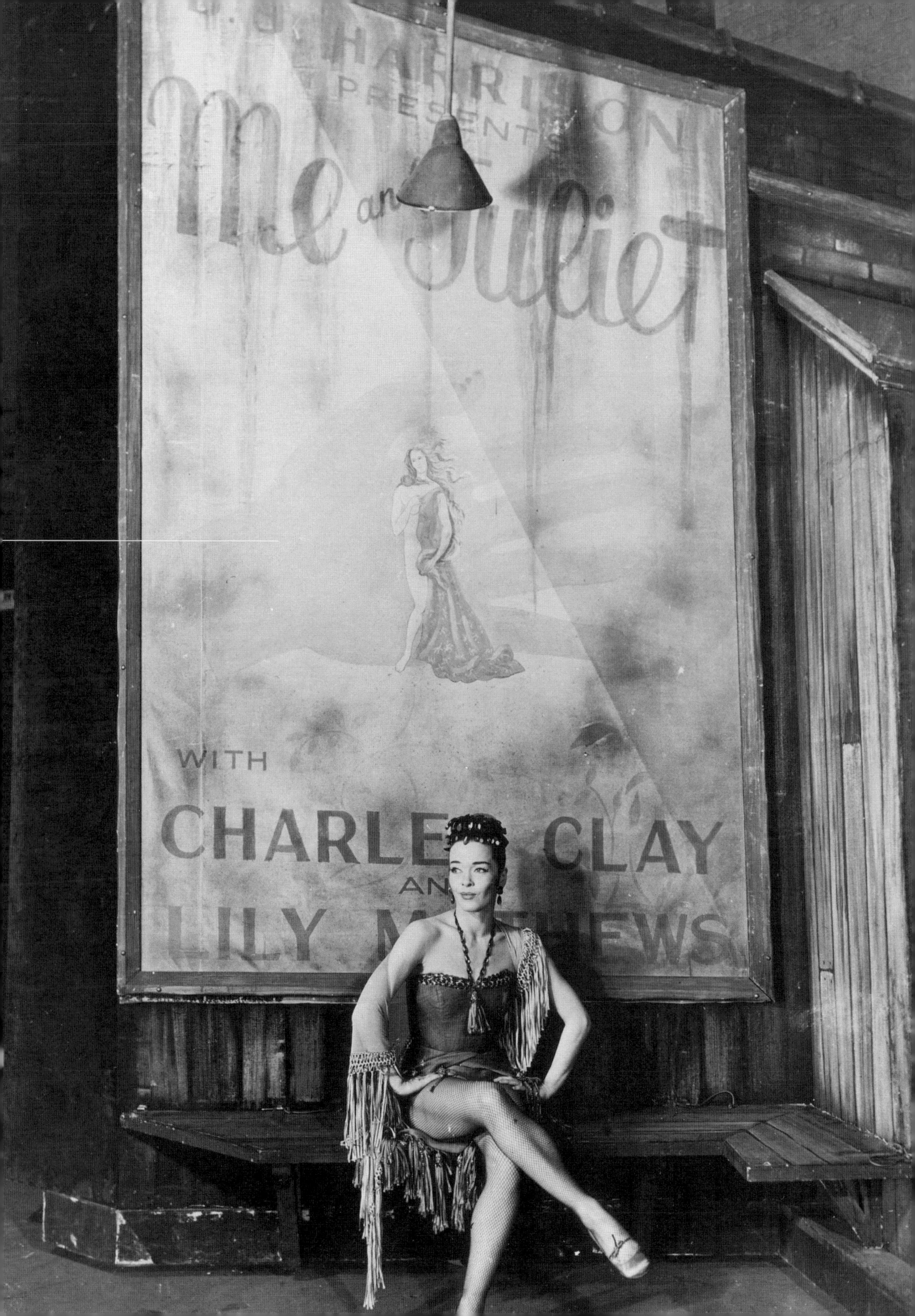
PRESENTS
Juliet
WITH
CLAY

# NO OTHER LOVE

Lyrics by OSCAR HAMMERSTEIN II

Music by RICHARD RODGERS

Copyright © 1953 by Richard Rodgers and Oscar Hammerstein II
Copyright Renewed
WILLIAMSON MUSIC owner of publication and allied rights throughout the world
International Copyright Secured   All Rights Reserved

PIPE DREAM

*Pipe Dream* based on the novel *Sweet Thursday* by John Steinbeck. *Pipe Dream* opened on Broadway on November 30, 1955, at the Shubert Theatre for a run of 246 performances.

Music by Richard Rodgers. Book and Lyrics by Oscar Hammerstein II. Directed by Harold Clurman. Choreography by Boris Runanin. Orchestrations by Robert Russell Bennett. Musical director, Salvatore Dell'Isola. Produced by Rodgers and Hammerstein.

## PRINCIPAL ORIGINAL CAST

| | |
|---|---|
| Fauna | Helen Traubel |
| Doc | William Johnson |
| Suzy | Judy Tyler |
| Hazel | Mike Kellin |
| Mac | G. D. Wallace |

**SYNOPSIS.** This story of drifters and bums takes place in Cannery Row, in Monterey on the California coast. Suzy, a vagrant arrested for stealing food, is taken in by a big-hearted madam named Fauna, who runs the bordello, the Bear Flag "Cafe." Doc, a marine biologist, is a local hero of sorts among the drifters. Suzy falls in love with him. Doc's friends try to urge along the matchmaking with little success. After Doc's arm is mysteriously broken, Suzy nurses him back to health, and he realizes that he's in love with her.

**COMMENTARY.** John Steinbeck, a longtime friend of both Rodgers and Hammerstein, had once attempted to adapt his Cannery Row stories as a musical for the stage, but the project never took off. Instead he wrote a novel, *Sweet Thursday,* based on characters from the original stories. It was Steinbeck who approached Rodgers and Hammerstein about the musicalization that resulted in *Pipe Dream.*

Just as *Pipe Dream* was going into rehearsal, Richard Rodgers was diagnosed with cancer of the jaw, and surgery was performed shortly thereafter. As a result, he was forced to spend three weeks away from the show, recovering well enough to join the production for the out-of-town opening in New Haven.

*Pipe Dream* had the shortest Broadway run of any Rodgers and Hammerstein musical (until their posthumous *State Fair* in 1996). Rodgers explained, "We had simply gone too far away from what was expected. People were unwilling to accept the show on its own terms. It had to be compared with our other works and that indefinable thing called "the Rodgers and Hammerstein image." Had we been a couple of unknowns, I'm convinced that *Pipe Dream* would have been better received. Which is not to say that it was an unflawed gem; far from it."

p. 135: Helen Traubel in a scene from the original 1955 Broadway production of *Pipe Dream.*

p. 136: ABOVE: Helen Traubel as Fauna and Judy Tyler as Suzy in the 1955 Broadway production. BELOW: Mike Kellin as Hazel in the 1955 Broadway production.

# ALL AT ONCE YOU LOVE HER

Lyrics by OSCAR HAMMERSTEIN II

Music by RICHARD RODGERS

Copyright © 1955 by Richard Rodgers and Oscar Hammerstein II
Copyright Renewed
WILLIAMSON MUSIC owner of publication and allied rights throughout the world
International Copyright Secured   All Rights Reserved

dream will take pos - ses - sion of your heart. _____

**Refrain** *(slowly, with expression)*

You start to light her cig - ar -

ette And all at once you

love her. You've scarce - ly talked,

CINDERELLA

*Cinderella* (television) adapted from the fairy tale
"Cendrillon, ou la Petite Pantoufle de Vair" by Charles
Perrault. *Cinderella* was broadcast live on the CBS television
network at 8:00 p.m. (EST) on March 31, 1957.

Music by Richard Rodgers. Book and Lyrics by Oscar Ham-
merstein II. Directed by Ralph Nelson. Choreography by
Jonathan Lucas. Orchestrations by Robert Russell Bennett.
Musical director, Alfredo Antonini.

## PRINCIPAL ORIGINAL CAST

Cinderella . . . . . . . . . . . . . . . . . . . . . . . . . . . . Julie Andrews
The Prince . . . . . . . . . . . . . . . . . . . . . . . . . . . Jon Cypher
The Stepmother . . . . . . . . . . . . . . . . . . . . . . . Ilka Chase
Stepsister Portia . . . . . . . . . . . . . . . . . . . . . Kaye Ballard
Stepsister Joy . . . . . . . . . . . . . . . . . . . . . . Alice Ghostly
The Godmother . . . . . . . . . . . . . . . . . . . . . . Edith Adams

**SYNOPSIS.** Poor Cinderella is treated like a despised live-in
maid by her mean stepmother and stepsisters. The royal
palace announces that the Prince is giving a ball and that he is
hoping to meet his future bride among the guests. Cinderella,
forbidden to attend by her stepmother, is granted an impossi-
ble wish-come-true to attend the splendid affair by her godmother and by magic is transformed into a dazzlingly
adorned beauty, complete with coach and carriage. The Prince
and Cinderella fall in love at first sight, but she suddenly
departs just before the magic spell expires at midnight when
her finery will transform back into her customary shabby
clothes. In her haste she accidentally steps out of a glass slipper, which the Prince finds. He searches every household for
his mysterious love, trying the slipper on every young lady.
When Cinderella's foot fits perfectly, much to the horror of
her hateful family, the happily-ever-after ending is ensured.

**p. 141:** Julie Andrews in the title role of *Cinderella,* from
the original 1957 CBS television broadcast.

**p. 142:** ABOVE: Julie Andrews with Jon Cypher as the Prince
in a rehearsal for the 1957 television broadcast. RIGHT: Julie
Andrews in a scene from *Cinderella.*

**p. 143:** Brandy as Cinderella in the 1997 television version
aired on "The Wonderful World of Disney," ABC-TV.

**COMMENTARY.** The idea for a television musical of the *Cinderella* story originated with CBS executives in the summer of 1956 in response to the huge success of *Peter Pan* on NBC, which had starred Mary Martin. Earlier that same year Julie Andrews had emerged as the "toast of Broadway" in *My Fair Lady,* and CBS was convinced that she would be the perfect star for a new television musical. It was Ms. Andrews's agent who approached Rodgers and Hammerstein with the proposition of writing a musicalization of the fairy tale for her. "It was," Rodgers wrote in his autobiography, "right from the start."

Rodgers and Hammerstein wrote more than twenty-two songs for the score, some via long-distance correspondence when Oscar and his wife Dorothy were visiting Australia for several weeks to attend the 1956 Olympic Games. After all the necessary cuts, the writers only retained a handful of songs for the show.

According to CBS, more than 107 million people watched the live broadcast of *Cinderella* on March 31, 1957, the largest television audience ever up to that time. That night Julie Andrews became a household name in America. In 1965, CBS produced a new, color version of *Cinderella,* which was preserved on videotape and re-broadcast many times over the years. Lesley Ann Warren starred in the title role, and the noteworthy cast included Ginger Rogers, Celeste Holm, and Walter Pidgeon. In 1997, a new filmed version of the musical was produced for television and aired on "The Wonderful World of Disney" on ABC. Pop star Brandy starred as the title character, with Whitney Houston as her godmother. Bernadette Peters, Whoopi Goldberg, Jason Alexander, and Victor Garber were also featured in the all-star cast. Rodgers and Hammerstein's *Cinderella* has also lived happily-ever-after onstage, from opera houses to summer stock theaters.

# IN MY OWN LITTLE CORNER

Lyrics by OSCAR HAMMERSTEIN II

Music by RICHARD RODGERS

Copyright © 1957 by Richard Rodgers and Oscar Hammerstein II
Copyright Renewed
WILLIAMSON MUSIC owner of publication and allied rights throughout the world
International Copyright Secured   All Rights Reserved

145

146

# DO I LOVE YOU BECAUSE YOU'RE BEAUTIFUL?

Lyrics by OSCAR HAMMERSTEIN II

Music by RICHARD RODGERS

Copyright © 1957 by Richard Rodgers and Oscar Hammerstein II
Copyright Renewed
WILLIAMSON MUSIC owner of publication and allied rights throughout the world
International Copyright Secured   All Rights Reserved

Julie Andrews with Richard Rodgers and Oscar Hammerstein II on the set of
*Cinderella*, March 28, 1957.

# THERE'S MUSIC IN YOU

Lyrics by OSCAR HAMMERSTEIN II

Music by RICHARD RODGERS

Copyright © 1952 (Renewed) by Richard Rodgers and Oscar Hammerstein II
This version incorporates words and music from "ONE FOOT, OTHER FOOT," music by Richard Rodgers, lyrics by Oscar Hammerstein II
Copyright © 1947 (Renewed) by Richard Rodgers and Oscar Hammerstein II
For this version, Copyright © 1997 by Family Trust u/w Dorothy F. Rodgers, Family Trust u/w Richard Rodgers and The Estate of Oscar Hammerstein II
Williamson Music owner of publication and allied rights throughout the world
International Copyright Secured   All Rights Reserved

156

FLOWER DRUM
SONG

*Flower Drum Song* based on the novel *The Flower Drum Song* by C. Y. Lee. *Flower Drum Song* opened on Broadway on December 1, 1958, at the St. James Theatre for a run of six hundred performances.

Music by Richard Rodgers. Lyrics by Oscar Hammerstein II. Book by Oscar Hammerstein II and Joseph Fields. Directed by Gene Kelly. Choreography by Carol Haney. Orchestrations by Robert Russell Bennett. Musical director, Salvatore Dell'Isola. Produced by Rodgers and Hammerstein, in association with Joseph Fields.

## PRINCIPAL ORIGINAL CAST

Mei Li . . . . . . . . . . . . . . . . . . . . . . . . . . . . . . . . . . . . . . . . Miyoshi Umeki
Linda Low . . . . . . . . . . . . . . . . . . . . . . . . . . . . . . . . . . . . . . Pat Suzuki
Madam Liang . . . . . . . . . . . . . . . . . . . . . . . . . . . . . . . . . . . Juanita Hall
Wang Ta . . . . . . . . . . . . . . . . . . . . . . . . . . . . . . . . . . . . . . . Ed Kenney
Sammy Fong . . . . . . . . . . . . . . . . . . . . . . . . . . . . . . . . . . Larry Blyden
Helen Chao . . . . . . . . . . . . . . . . . . . . . . . . . . . . . . . . . Arabella Hong
Wang Chi Yang . . . . . . . . . . . . . . . . . . . . . . . . . . . . . . . . . Keye Luke

**SYNOPSIS.** Mei Li, a shy young Chinese mail-order bride, has recently arrived in San Francisco's Chinatown to marry Sammy Fong. However, Sammy is more interested in Linda Low, the star of the show in the nightclub he owns, and has no desire to enter into this arranged marriage to Mei Li. He sells the marriage contract to Mr. Wang, a Chinese gentleman of the old school, who is looking for an appropriate bride for his son, Wang Ta, who happens to also be infatuated with Linda. Mei Li's father insists that the original marriage contract with Sammy be honored, but by this time Wang Ta realizes that he actually is in love with Mei Li rather than the profligate Linda. Mei Li provides a happy solution when she declares that since she entered the country illegally, the marriage contract with Sammy is null and void. This leaves Sammy free for Linda, and Mei Li is free to follow her own heart and marry Wang Ta.

**COMMENTARY.** After the success of the fairy tale *Cinderella*, Rodgers and Hammerstein returned to familiar topics already explored in both *South Pacific* and *The King and I*: the problems between people of different cultural backgrounds and different generations. *Flower Drum Song* contrasted the traditions of first-generation Chinese immigrants living in San Francisco and their American-born children.

Reflecting the American setting, several numbers display a strong, jazzy idiom; other songs, however, have an Asian flavor (though they remain Rodgers through-and-through) and in instrumentation even employ percussion instruments rarely heard from a Broadway pit orchestra. Hammerstein's lyrics for certain numbers echo Far Eastern cultures in their sensitive reflection. "I Am Going to Like It Here," for instance, is written as a *pantoum*, a sophisticated form of Malayan poetry.

*Flower Drum Song* enjoyed a healthy run of nearly eighteen months. A London edition opened in London on March 24, 1960, and ran for 464 performances. A film version was released in 1961. Though at this writing it has yet to have a Broadway revival, *Flower Drum Song* endures as one of Rodgers and Hammerstein's most delicately fashioned musicals. It is a rich piece of lyric theater that deserves rediscovery.

**p. 157:** Miyoshi Umeki as Mei Li in the original 1958 Broadway production of *Flower Drum Song*.

**p. 158:** TOP LEFT: "A Hundred Million Miracles": Keye Luke as Wang Chi Yang and Juanita Hall as Madam Liang with Miyoshi Umeki. BOTTOM LEFT: Larry Blyden as Sammy Fong with Miyoshi Umeki. BOTTOM RIGHT: A scene from the original production of *Flower Drum Song*.

**p. 159:** ABOVE: Ed Kenney as Wang Ta with Miyoshi Umeki. RIGHT: a scene from the original Broadway production.

# A HUNDRED MILLION MIRACLES

Lyrics by OSCAR HAMMERSTEIN II

Music by RICHARD RODGERS

Copyright © 1958 by Richard Rodgers and Oscar Hammerstein II
Copyright Renewed
WILLIAMSON MUSIC owner of publication and allied rights throughout the world
International Copyright Secured   All Rights Reserved

# LOVE, LOOK AWAY

Lyrics by OSCAR HAMMERSTEIN II

Music by RICHARD RODGERS

**Lento**

I have wished be - fore. I will wish no

**Moderato espressivo**
**Refrain**

more. Love, look a - way! _____ Love, look a - way from

me. Fly, when you pass my door, Fly and get lost at

Copyright © 1958 by Richard Rodgers and Oscar Hammerstein II
Copyright Renewed
WILLIAMSON MUSIC owner of publication and allied rights throughout the world
International Copyright Secured   All Rights Reserved

# YOU ARE BEAUTIFUL

Lyrics by OSCAR HAMMERSTEIN II

Music by RICHARD RODGERS

Copyright © 1958 by Richard Rodgers and Oscar Hammerstein II
Copyright Renewed
WILLIAMSON MUSIC owner of publication and allied rights throughout the world
International Copyright Secured   All Rights Reserved

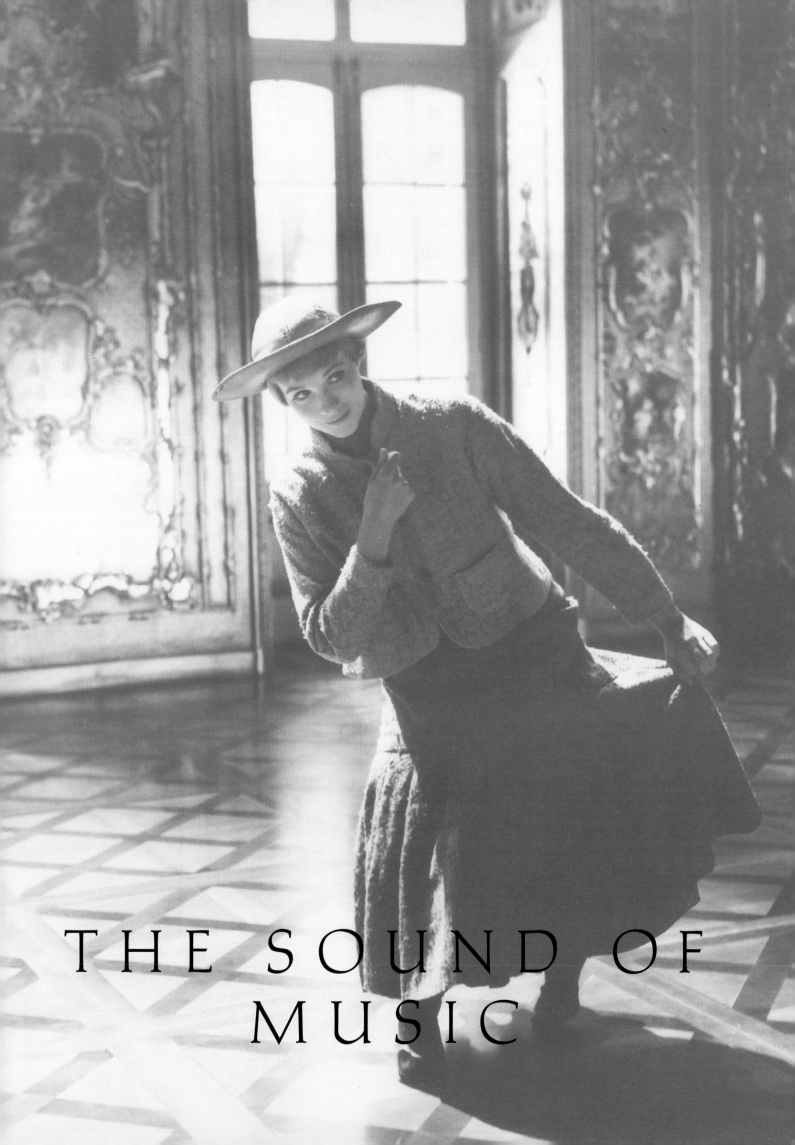

# THE SOUND OF
# MUSIC

*The Sound of Music* suggested by the book *The Story of the Trapp Family Singers* by Maria Augusta Trapp. *The Sound of Music* opened on Broadway on November 16, 1959, at the Lunt-Fontanne Theatre for a run of 1,443 performances.

Music by Richard Rodgers. Lyrics by Oscar Hammerstein II. Book by Howard Lindsay and Russel Crouse. Directed by Vincent J. Donehue. Orchestrations by Robert Russell Bennett. Musical director, Frederick Dvonch. Produced by Leland Hayward, Richard Halliday, Rodgers and Hammerstein.

## PRINCIPAL ORIGINAL CAST

| | |
|---|---|
| Maria Rainer | Mary Martin |
| Captain Georg von Trapp | Theodore Bikel |
| The Mother Abbess | Patricia Neway |
| Elsa Schraeder | Marion Marlowe |
| Max Detweiler | Kurt Kasznar |
| Liesl | Lauri Peters |
| Rolf Gruber | Brian Davies |

**SYNOPSIS.** The story is set in Austria, 1938. Maria is a high-spirited young postulant at Nonnberg Abbey. The wise Mother Abbess senses that Maria may be unready for life as a nun and sends her to serve as governess to the seven children of widower Captain von Trapp. She soon wins the children over and teaches them music. Though the Captain is engaged to Baroness Schraeder, he and Maria fall in love and marry. The Nazis take control of Austria while the couple is away on their honeymoon. After the family makes a concert appearance at a music festival, they make a narrow escape from the Nazi tyranny in their beloved homeland to the safety of Switzerland.

**COMMENTARY.** The partnership of Rodgers and Hammerstein ended with a glorious swan song in *The Sound of Music*. The idea for the show began with Mary Martin, who had seen a German film about the Trapp Family Singers. Initially, Martin envisioned the story as a dramatic play with music inserted and asked Rodgers and Hammerstein to contribute one song. They liked the story, but disagreed with the approach, concluding that it would be stronger as a new musical with an original score. Martin loved the suggestion, but only if Rodgers and Hammerstein would write the show. At the time they were in the middle of writing *Flower Drum Song;* Martin and her producers agreed to wait until the writers were available.

Because Howard Lindsay and Russel Crouse had already been signed on to the project as scriptwriters, Hammerstein's role, uncharacteristically, was confined to writing lyrics. Perhaps this lighter load was fortuitous because he was diagnosed with cancer just as the score to *The Sound of Music* was being finished. Hammerstein was too ill to go to New Haven for the out-of-town opening, but did join the company in Boston on its second stop. There he and Rodgers wrote their last song together, when "Edelweiss" was added to the production. Nine months after the show's Broadway premiere, Oscar Hammerstein II died at his farm in Doylestown, Pennsylvania. Rodgers later said of his partner's death, "Almost to the day he died everything about him was an affirmation of life. He was then in his sixty-sixth year, but he was infused with a faith and an optimism that only grew stronger as he grew older."

*The Sound of Music* opened in London on May 18, 1961, for a run of 2,385 performances and is the longest-running American musical in the theatrical history of the West End. The show also was produced in many foreign countries, receiving everywhere the same enthusiastic response. But it was the 1965 film version, starring Julie Andrews, which ensured forever the popularity of Rodgers and Hammerstein around the world. The film won the Academy Award for Best Picture and remains the most successful movie musical of all time. An enduring favorite on stage as well as screen, *The Sound of Music* returned to Broadway in 1998, starring Rebecca Luker.

**p. 173:** Julie Andrews as Maria Rainer in the 1965 film version of *The Sound of Music*.

**p. 174:** TOP LEFT: Rebecca Luker as Maria with the von Trapp children in the 1998 Broadway revival. TOP RIGHT: Mary Martin as Maria in the original 1959 Broadway production. BOTTOM: Mary Martin with Theodore Bikel as Captain George von Trapp in the original Broadway production.

**p. 175:** Rebecca Luker in the 1998 Broadway revival.

# MY FAVORITE THINGS

Lyrics by OSCAR HAMMERSTEIN II

Music by RICHARD RODGERS

Copyright © 1959 by Richard Rodgers and Oscar Hammerstein II
Copyright Renewed
WILLIAMSON MUSIC owner of publication and allied rights throughout the world
International Copyright Secured   All Rights Reserved

"So Long, Farewell": The von Trapp children in the 1998 Broadway revival played by (clockwise from left) Natalie Hall, Ryan Hopkins, Andrea Bowen, Sara Zelle, Matthew Ballinger, Tracy Alison Walsh, and Ashley Rose Orr.

# THE SOUND OF MUSIC

Lyrics by OSCAR HAMMERSTEIN II

Music by RICHARD RODGERS

My day in the hills has come to an end, I know. A star has come out to tell me it's time to go. But deep in the dark green shad-ows are

Copyright © 1959 by Richard Rodgers and Oscar Hammerstein II
Copyright Renewed
WILLIAMSON MUSIC owner of publication and allied rights throughout the world
International Copyright Secured   All Rights Reserved

# CLIMB EV'RY MOUNTAIN

Lyrics by OSCAR HAMMERSTEIN II

Music by RICHARD RODGERS

**Maestoso**

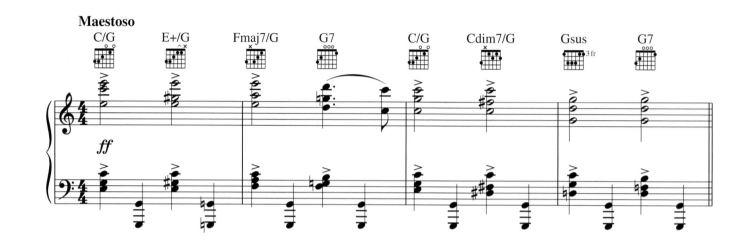

**Refrain** *(with deep feeling, like a prayer)*

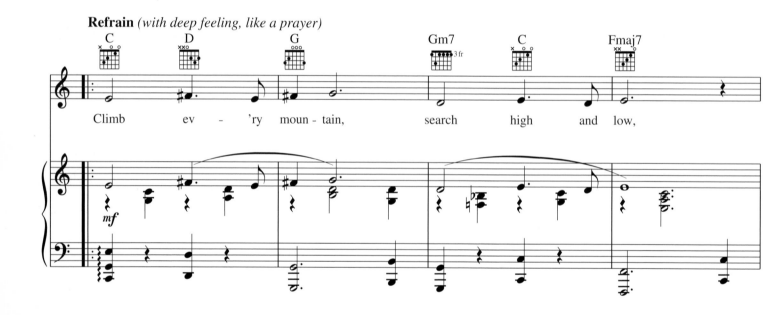

Climb ev - 'ry moun - tain, search high and low,

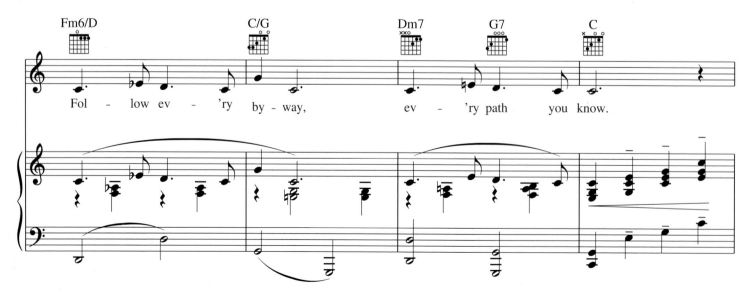

Fol - low ev - 'ry by - way, ev - 'ry path you know.

Copyright © 1959 by Richard Rodgers and Oscar Hammerstein II
Copyright Renewed
WILLIAMSON MUSIC owner of publication and allied rights throughout the world
International Copyright Secured   All Rights Reserved

188

Mary Martin as Maria with the von Trapp children in the original 1959
Broadway production.

# EDELWEISS

Lyrics by OSCAR HAMMERSTEIN II

Music by RICHARD RODGERS

Copyright © 1959 by Richard Rodgers and Oscar Hammerstein II
Copyright Renewed
WILLIAMSON MUSIC owner of publication and allied rights throughout the world
International Copyright Secured   All Rights Reserved

192